WHAT PEOPLE ARE SAYING ABOUT JEREMY ROSAS AND *HOW TO UNLOCK GOD'S VOICE*

"I am so happy to recommend this amazing book. Jeremy speaks words that will bring life and encouragement to you. Your life will be revolutionized and changed, and you will never be the same. I have been his pastor since he was six, and he has not wavered. He remains focused on the call of God for his life. So, enjoy, and be blessed."

Roy Love
Senior Pastor, Praise Chapel

———— ❦ ————

I0111955

"We receive many invitations in this life, and there's almost always a moment of decision when we have to RSVP and either decline or accept what has been offered to us. What we find in Jeremy Rosas' book, *How to Unlock God's Voice: 30 Days of Fire,* is an invitation that hungry hearts will want to accept—to go on a journey to become better acquainted with the voice of God. Jeremy provides a 30-day 'map' to help the reader navigate this adventure that will hopefully continue on after the last page is read. He provides 30 strategic 'keys' designed to help you recognize and respond to the Spirit of God whenever He is speaking to you.

I believe this book will be a great aid in your walk with the Lord if your 'RSVP' to His invitation to know Him better is a forever yes."

Dr. Roberts Liardon
Author, God's Generals series

"Jeremy Rosas is one of the 'now generation' voices that God has amplified for this hour in history. Through his new book, you'll be inspired to believe and trust for God's best as Jeremy shares what has been revealed to him during his time of study and prayer. Jeremy's passion is to know more of God and motivate others to do the same. This book will do precisely that."

Pastor Tony Suarez
Founder of Revivalmakers Ministries
www.revivalmakers.org

"God's voice changes everything. When He spoke in the beginning, He released divine light into the darkness and created divine life in the universe. The world and everything in it was formed by His voice. Whenever He spoke to the ancients throughout Scriptures, His voice brought divine instruction, guidance, courage, healing, deliverance, or a vast array of other divine manifestations.

"For Moses, this voice came from a burning bush. For the Hebrew children, this voice appeared in the midst of the flaming furnace. For you and me, we can still hear God's voice today!

The ability to hear God's voice has shaped my personal life and ministry, and it is a vital key in the life of every believer. If we desire to unlock the best and most vibrant life that God has planned for us to live, we must hear His voice.

"God wants us to live in the fire of His voice, and that's one of the reasons I'm so delighted that Jeremy Rosas has written this powerful devotional, *How To Unlock God's Voice: 30 Days of Fire!* As you read this book, your spirit will be stirred, and your heart will be opened to hear the voice of God with greater clarity!

Don't rush through the pages. Instead, allow the wisdom keys God has given to Jeremy to be imparted into your life, and you will discover that they open the door to greater encounters and Holy Spirit fire!"

Joshua Mills
International Glory Ministries
Bestselling Author, Moving in Glory Realms
www.joshuamills.com

How To Unlock God's Voice

McDougal & Associates
Servants of Christ and Stewards of the Mysteries of God

HOW TO UNLOCK GOD'S VOICE

30 DAYS OF FIRE!

by

Jeremy Rosas

Unless otherwise noted, all Scripture quotations are from *The Holy Bible, English Standard Version*, copyright © 2001 by Crossway Bibles, a publishing ministry of Good News Publishers. References marked NLT are from *The Holy Bible, New Living Translation*, copyright © 1996, 2004, 2007 by Tyndale House Foundation. Used by permission of Tyndale House Publishers, Inc., Carol Stream, Illinois. References marked NIV are from *The Holy Bible, New International Version,* copyright © 1973, 1978, 1984 by International Bible Society, Colorado Springs, Colorado. References marked NKJV are from *The Holy Bible, New King James Version*, copyright © 1979, 1980, 1982, by Thomas Nelson, Inc., Nashville, Tennessee. References marked BSB are from the Berean Study Bible © 2016, 2018 by Bible Hub. References marked NASB are from the New American Standard Bible, copyright © 1960, 1962, 1963, 1968, 1971, 1972, 1973, 1975, 1977 by the Lockman Foundation, La Habra, California. All rights reserved. Used by permission.

Published by:

McDougal & Associates
18896 Greenwell Springs Road
Greenwell Springs, LA 70739
www.thepublishedword.com

McDougal & Associates is dedicated to the spreading of the Gospel of Jesus Christ to as many people as possible in the shortest time possible.

ISBN 978-1-950398-54-6

Printed on demand in the U.S., the U.K., Australia and the UAE
For Worldwide Distribution

DEDICATION

This book is dedicated to God and for the purpose of bringing *you* closer to Him. He has amazing plans for you, and He wants to show you how real He is.

CONTENTS

Foreword by Marcos Witt

God has always had a people. Even in the darkest of times, He's never failed to provide us with powerful voices that speak truth, encouragement, hope, and mercy through Christ our Savior. Every generation is born with prophets, teachers, evangelists, pastors, apostles, and men and women of God He uses to signal The Way, encouraging people to know and experience His beautiful presence in a personal way. Each one of these anointed servants delivers their message in unique and creative ways, some through music, others in preaching and teaching, and yet others through writing or expressive arts, poetry, video, and movie making.

Throughout the ages, God has always raised up voices to speak into hearts and minds, with a language that is understandable to that particular generation. The message never changes, however the way it is communicated MUST change in order to be relevant to the times in which each generation lives. One of the voices God has raised up to speak into his generation is Jeremy Rosas. From the first day I met him, his passion for God was very clear. As a very young man, he began to press into God, learning, listening, serving, and giving his time and effort to bless the people of God in his local church and abroad.

As the years have passed, I've observed Jeremy's spiritual maturity and commitment to God's Word, and there's no doubt in my mind the Lord will use him as one of the holy mouthpieces to prophesy to dry bones and bring life where there seems to be none.

Faithfulness is one of the greatest keys to be used by God. In fact, God only promotes the faithful. I am impressed with how Jeremy is still faithful to his local church and his pastor, serving when and where he is needed. From my perspective, this is one of the reasons God is raising him up as an anointed voice to his generation.

In this 30-day devotional, Jeremy has organized his thoughts around a series of one word chapters (except for chapters 11 and 30, which have three). With simple examples and ease of language, he encourages us to unlock God's voice in our life. In each of these brief teachings, we are encouraged and spurred on in our faith. We fall back in love with Jesus. We are taught, refreshed, and edified with great scriptures, and, at times, curious and humorous but inspired illustrations.

As you open this devotional, ask the Holy Spirit to speak to you. Approach each lesson with a teachable spirit. The Lord always surprises us with new understanding and fresh knowledge of God's wisdom, as we are willing to listen to His voice. Make yourself available to the Word of God as Jeremy Rosas leads us through these 30 days of unlocking the voice of God in our lives.

Anticipating great things,
Marcos Witt
The Woodlands, Texas
January 2022

But when you pray, go into your room and shut the door and pray to your Father who is in secret. And your Father who sees in secret will reward you.
— Matthew 6:6

INTRODUCTION

Hearing the voice of God is not easily defined—and it never will be—but there are tools, characteristics, and mentalities that will lead you there. The voice of God can come in many forms. He can speak audibly, internally, visually, physically, and to any degree He sees fit to communicate with you.

It's important to not limit how God can speak to you. The ability to hear God's voice must be trained and developed. There is a level of clarity that comes through your level of surrender to God. Similarly to a relationship with anyone in life, the more you invest time in and with a person, the easier it is to recognize that person's voice, their characteristics, and manner of doing things. The same principle applies with God. As you increase your time with Him, as you make the right decisions, as you pursue Him, and as you increase the level with which you pursue Him, so also it will become easier and clearer to recognize His voice, how He works, how He speaks, and how He interacts with you.

In this thirty-day journey, focus and set your mind and your attention on becoming intimate with God. Take every topic and make it a daily habit to apply it to your relationship with God and your passion for Him. Enjoy the journey, and make it a lifestyle.

Jeremy Rosas

DESPERATION

You must become desperate. When you want something badly enough, you'll go to any degree to obtain it. A necessary quality to develop the voice of God in your life, desperation will fuel you when you don't feel like making the effort required. When you feel lost and hopeless, desperation causes things to change. When you learn how to harness and create a state of positive desperation, you can push yourself to pursue God when you might not be having the best day, when things didn't go your way, and even in the middle of the biggest storms in your life.

Storms are something that we all encounter, but it's important to know the voice of the One who can silence and remove those storms. That's where desperation comes in. Your ability to trust God on your best day, as well as on your worst day, will make you consistent. It will make you faithful. You must develop the mentality that you will have an intimate relationship with God — at all costs.

This is the same quality the woman with the issue of blood had when she saw Jesus. She fought and forced her way through crowds. She got dirty, and she didn't care what people thought of her. Why? Because she knew who Jesus was and what He was capable of. Her circumstances created her desperation. You must develop a greater skill: the ability to become desperate regardless of your circumstances.

Desperation does not have to be a negative quality, and it doesn't have to be created by a negative situation. Desperation led this woman to an encounter with Jesus that forever changed her life, and it became a moment forever marked in time—one glorious moment of desperation! In the same way, your desperation for God—your deep desire for Him—will lead to many encounters with God and a greater realization of how much He loves you and how much He wants to speak to you.

In fact, God's desire for you is greater than you ever thought was possible. So today, become like that woman. Claw your way through the "crowd!" Shut off the thoughts that try to clutter your mind! Forget about the problems at work, and take a moment away from the busyness of life. Create a mentality of desperation, and then continue to develop that desperation. Eat, breathe, drink, and consume the quality of desperation, but direct that desperation in one direction—toward God and His voice.

INFORMATION

Information is a necessity of life. *Information* can be defined as "facts that are provided or learned about something or someone." To know the voice of God you must first know God. It is important to understand that God is more important than His voice. The main goal should not be His voice. The main goal should always be Him.

When you make a relationship with God your top priority, His voice will follow. It's like getting to know someone. You ask them questions, you spend time with them, and you get to know them. You're taking in loads of information, and your mind begins to process everything. The more time you invest in that person the more you recognize their voice, their qualities, their likes, their dislikes, what they love, and what they hate. You discover who they are.

Likewise, God, in His infinite wisdom, knew that we would need information about Him so that we could know Him. This information begins with my favorite book in the world—the Bible. The Bible contains stories, teachings, lessons, and the blueprints that reveal to you who God is. As you read the Bible, something happens. The Bible says, in John 1:1, *"In the beginning was the Word, and the Word was with God, and the Word was God."* The Word was God! So, when you read the Bible, you're reading

God, you're discovering God, and you're actually spending time with God.

The same way you build a relationship with any person, spending time with them, you are doing the exact same thing with God when you read the Bible. Constant Bible reading keeps you focused, and it causes your mind, eyes, and ears to be opened to what God is speaking, saying, and doing in your life.

The Bible is the first source of information that is necessary to developing the voice of God in your life. The Bible itself says, *"Faith comes by hearing, and hearing by the word of God"* (Romans 10:17, NKJV). So the faith that says that God can speak to you and wants to speak to you can only be released when you HEAR the WORD of God.

As you read the Bible, God is supernaturally constructing a platform in your life that He can build on and work with. An increase of information will lead to an increase of clarity and understanding of how and when He speaks. So dig into the Bible. Make it a constant. Devour it! As you increase your time in the Bible, God will increase the degree to which He speaks to you.

DAY 3

TRANSFORMATION

God wants to transform you, but it's important to know exactly what He wants to transform you into. To transform something is to alter it—to change it. Make yourself available to change. Don't fight it. Regardless of where you are in life with God, whether a brand-new Christian, a long-term Christian, a tired Christian, or perhaps you're a non-Christian reading this, God never stops transforming you. You never reach the end of the line of growth with God. He's always looking to make you better.

One of the keys to having a powerful relationship with God is allowing Him to constantly mold you and make you into who He wants you to be. You must be teachable, correctable, and disciplined. It is equally necessary to have these qualities in order to hear His voice. There's a reward when you pay the price. So what is that price? The Bible says, in Romans 12:2 (NLT), *"Don't copy the behavior and customs of this world, but let God transform you into a new person by changing the way you think. Then you will learn to know God's will for you, which is good and pleasing and perfect."* The key word here is TRANSFORM.

God's goal for you is to look like His Son, not like the world. In order to understand this verse, you have to examine the one right before it. It says, *"And so, dear brothers and sisters, I plead with you to give your bodies to God because of all He has done for you. Let them be a living and holy sacrifice—the kind He will find acceptable. This is truly the way to worship Him,"* (Romans 12:1, NLT). We are to make our lives a sacrifice to God. To sacrifice yourself spiritually to God is to allow Him to burn away every part of you that He doesn't like: wrong habits, wrong desires, wrong friendships, etc. If you maintain a mindset of being yielded to what and who God wants for your life, you are allowing Him to transform you.

Sometimes we may think that God's voice can only be heard audibly or as a loud thought in our mind, but there's much more to it. Training yourself to recognize God's voice involves being willing to respond to His nudging. Nudging is one of the ways God speaks. The impression to let go of an old lifestyle, the quickening to get rid of an old habit or addiction, the knot in your stomach when you feel you shouldn't be in a certain environment are all the nudgings from God. As you allow God to dictate what you do in life and how you do it, His voice will become stronger and clearer.

DAY 4

PERSPIRATION

We all know what it is to perspire, to work hard, and to run after something. We know the benefits of the reward system: what you put in, you get out. Perspiration, or sweat, is the proof of that effort, and it can also be a confirmation that good things are to come.

A good example of this is the process a woman goes through in giving birth to a child. It requires a time of waiting, the need for patience, painful and tiresome moments, and exhaustion. It's a process that no one would ever want to go through, but there's a great reward for making it to the end. The last step in pregnancy is the labor stage, where much perspiration is required. Sweat is a sign that the baby is coming. Likewise, in your pursuit of God and of hearing His voice, sweat can be a sign that His voice is coming.

You can desire God so badly that you do exactly that—sweat. There have been several times in my alone times with God that I put my headphones on and went after Him so strongly in my time of worship that I ended up perspiring. It's like working out, running, or playing a sport, but in this case, my goal is God and to hear His voice.

God will reward you for pursuing Him. When you work diligently and profusely toward a specific goal, you get results that are favorable; but hard work and perspiration are essential. Get out of your comfort zone in your alone time with God. Do something out of the ordinary. Dare to believe that God is physically there waiting for you and looking to reward you. The Bible says it like this, *"And it is impossible to please God without faith. Anyone who wants to come to Him must believe that God exists and that He rewards those who sincerely seek Him,"* (Hebrews 11:6, NLT).

So, be expectant! Dig deep! Become passionate for God! The greatest accomplishments, destinies, callings, and victories in life will all come after moments of perspiring.

DAY 5

SACRIFICE

It's important that you know the significance of the sacrifice that was made for you to hear God's voice. You will never hear God's voice because you deserve it, but you can always hear God's voice because Jesus earned it. One of the hardest things to accept in the Kingdom of God is the fact that you don't deserve the right to be there. You have to realize that you're accepted, entitled, blessed, provided for, and cared for, but only because Jesus paid for your right to have those things. It's like getting a free ticket with all expenses paid. You did nothing, but you inherit everything.

Jesus lived a sacrificial lifestyle and was constantly surrendered to God, His Father. There was a complete willingness in Jesus to have no will of His own. There was a tenacity to please the Father at all costs. The sacrifice that Jesus made, the blood He spilled, the sweat He released, and the moments of bitterness and agony were all for one outcome: so that you and I could have an intimate relationship with the Father.

Jesus lived so perfectly that His sacrifice forever became your freedom. You have free access to the Father, the Son, Jesus, and the Holy Spirit because of one Man. In order for you to thrive in your relationship with God, it is essential to realize that Jesus gave absolutely everything for you to be able to hear the voice of God. Without Jesus, you would have to earn your right to hear God—and that's impossible. Because of Jesus, a relationship with God will forever be your free gift. All you have to do is open it.

DAY 6

LOVE

Hearing and obeying the voice of God will make you realize how much He truly loves you. You won't pursue someone you don't love, and you can't fully love someone until you've known them. It took me a little while, in my walk with God, to realize how much He actually loves me. In fact, it took a heartbreak.

I was twenty-three years old, and I had only a few years of experience in hearing God's voice when I faced one of the hardest battles of my life. One of the greatest things God has taught me from hearing His voice is to trust Him when He speaks. I had a moment when there was a particular girl I liked, and after learning that she liked me too, my next move was to ask her out. On my way to ask her I had a sick feeling in my stomach, and I felt God tugging at me to ask Him if He even wanted me to date this girl. I pulled the car over to pray, and I heard God telling me a very strong "NO" in response to dating her. Initially, I listened, and I went on to tell the girl I couldn't date her.

Fast forward a few weeks, and I found myself talking to the girl and beginning to like her more, to the point that I disobeyed God and went out with her anyway. This disobedience lasted six months ... until the relationship took a nasty hit, and I got hurt badly. I was so hurt that I could feel my heart in pain, and I couldn't think straight.

On the first day of the heartbreak, I ran to my room where all the memories of the past six months, along with the reminders of God's voice and warnings and my disobedience, all came back to haunt me. I knew the only thing I could do was go back to God, but I felt dirty. I closed the door to my bedroom, fell to my knees and cried out to God in one statement, "God, I'm sorry for disobeying You. Please forgive me and have mercy on me."

Very quickly and subtly, I heard His voice. He said, "I love you." I immediately put my face to the ground and started crying. I felt so unworthy of His love. I screamed, "God, why do You love me? You knew I was going to disobey You, and You knew I was going to get hurt, and You tried to keep me from it. WHY DO YOU STILL WANT ME?"

For the next forty-five days I dedicated time to God more than I ever had before, and I discovered a love that no one could ever have offered me. I repented, came back to Him, and saw that He had never left me. I thought of everything Jesus did in the thirty-three years He spent here on Earth. I now saw it as an act of love, and it made me fall even more in love with Him. His love is profound, and hearing His voice will enhance your relationship with Him. Relationships will never grow if one person does all the talking. Listening for His voice will change everything.

HEART

The heart is composed of many things: likes, dislikes, traits, characteristics, qualities, decisions, passions, and hunger—to name a few. Your heart generally determines what you do in life, the decisions you make, and the directions you go. In fact, many people use the phrase, "follow your heart." It sounds nice, but when it comes to God, your heart cannot be your ruler, for it can also be misleading.

The Bible breaks it down like this, *"The heart is deceitful above all things, and desperately sick; who can understand it?"* (Jeremiah 17:9). One of the key elements in hearing God's voice is trusting Him with your heart by giving it to Him. Yes, this is key! When being asked what the most important commandment was, Jesus answered, *"You shall love the Lord your God with all your heart and with all your soul and with all your mind"* (Matthew 22:37). Don't aim to "sort of" love God; aim to give Him everything.

The only way you can love God with your whole heart is by relying on Him and trusting Him with the areas that the heart consists of. For example, let's look at career passions. Perhaps you have a goal of being a professional athlete or a lawyer, but one day God speaks to you about your career choices. He may nudge you, impressing on you in some way or even directly speaking to you. But what would you do if He suddenly revealed to you that He wanted you in a completely different field from what you were originally pursuing? Suddenly you're met with a circumstance where you have to decide if you're going to be faithful to God or if you're going to choose your own way.

This is just one scenario out of many that has to do with the heart. The question will always remain: can you love God with all your heart? If yes, then give Him every aspect that has to do with the heart. Trust Him with it. Let Him make the decisions. Let Him take control. He'll never steer you wrong.

DAY 8

MIND

Your mind is powerful, yet it tends to get in the way—unless, that is, you find a way to control it. Your mind will tell you that you're not really hearing God's voice; you're just hearing your own thoughts. It's important to refine the mind, to clean it, to shape it, to transform it. To love God with all your mind is the second facet that Jesus mentioned when speaking of the most important commandment.

Your ability to feed your mind the proper "food" will lead to clarity when it comes to hearing God's voice. A clear and sound mind will sharpen every aspect of your life. So, training your mind to love God is an essential part of being able to hear Him. The Bible gives us a beautiful word, *"Do not be conformed to this world, but be transformed by the renewal of your mind, that by testing you may discern what is the will of God, what is good and acceptable and perfect,"* (Romans 12:2). You can only be transformed when your mind has been renewed.

So, how can we feed the mind? The same way we've been feeding it for years, through our eyes and the ears. What you watch and what you hear begins to form your mind. In fact, a lot of the ways we think, process, and handle any matter is due to the manner in which we have formed our mind over the years. Music, TV, social media, books, relationships, friendships, and environments have all shaped us. Whether we believe it or not, we're shaped by what we entertain. We're molded by what we allow into our life.

To love God with all your mind is to allow God to tell you and to reveal to you what He deems is appropriate and good for you to let in. The world will try to train you and teach you that everything is allowed, that there are no consequences, and that "you need to be you." It's a thought that doesn't sound so bad on the surface, but this is the exact thought the devil would love for you to believe.

Jesus wasn't amazing and perfect because He did whatever He wanted; He was amazing and perfect because He always did what the Father wanted. The submissiveness of Jesus is found throughout the Bible, so why should we aim for anything less or think that we're exempt? There is a reward for sacrifice. There is a reward for paying the price that others aren't willing to pay. When you give up secular or worldly music that doesn't honor God, when you get rid of pornography, or when you stop watching movies that try to push the demonic realm on you, you're beginning to love God with all your mind. How? By rejecting and keeping your eyes and ears from what He would not want you to hear and see. He's looking for a generation that's different, a generation that isn't swayed by the world and that also doesn't look like the world, a different generation. He's looking for rebels for Jesus.

SOUL

The soul is fed by attraction. Who or what we give our time to begins to feed us. The soul was created with a longing for satisfaction and fulfillment, but it's important to give God that place. Unlocking God's voice will cause Him to become more attractive in your life.

There's a boost of confidence that comes when God speaks to you, and especially when a confirmation follows. Hearing God speak to you is proof that there's a relationship, and it will cause you to want more of Him, making you grow deeper and closer.

One of the most common references to the soul is found in the subject of soul-ties, which means strongly-knit relationships. This is a very delicate subject because relationships are easy to find and easy to start. It's also delicate because we can think we have the right to choose who can or cannot be part of our lives. Whether it be a friendship, a partnership in business, or whether it be who we date or marry, relationships are a huge part of our life. Throughout the Bible, we see that God supports relationships because this leads to growth and development.

This is the reason God told Noah to gather the animals for the ark in pairs. It's the reason that Jesus commanded His disciples to go in pairs to preach the Gospel in every village. It's the reason that God Himself, when looking at Adam in the book of Genesis, said, *"It is not good for the man to be alone. I will make a helper who is just right for him ... ,"* (Genesis 2:18, NLT). It's no mystery that more work can be done when there are two involved.

Take the ox, for example. One ox by itself has great strength and power, but when it is joined by another, the results will more than double. So, relationships are very important to God. What does this have to do with hearing His voice? It's another area God wants to trust you in. The greater He can trust you, the more He increases His voice in your life.

The way you can love God with your soul is by allowing Him to dictate who can be a part of your life. There are times when we will hear His voice or nudging, and there are times we need to use His wisdom. The Bible gives us two key verses to assist us:

1. *"Do not be misled: "Bad company corrupts good character,"* (1 Corinthians 15:33, NIV).

2. *"Do not be unequally yoked with unbelievers. For what partnership has righteousness with lawlessness? Or what fellowship has light with darkness?"* (2 Corinthians 6:14).

By getting to know people's lifestyles, habits, and convictions (or the lack thereof), you can generally tell if a particular person should be someone you spend time with or not. Analyze yourself. Who are the closest people to you? Who are you joined to? Are they making you better? Do they pull you away from God? Ask God to speak to you, to clear out anyone He may not want in your life, and to put in only those He wants. Love God, even with your soul.

CONCENTRATION

It's time to get focused! You have a great purpose in life. You're called to touch many, to heal many, to change many, to transform many, and to save many. You will overcome many obstacles and mountains. You will bring people closer to God. You will save people from the pits of Hell. Your calling is great, but without the voice of God being constant in your life, you'll never make a go of it. You'll miss it.

There are many souls who are waiting for you to break out of your shell, to become determined and tenacious in your walk with God, and to become aggressive. Your life, when you surrender to Jesus, becomes a burning flame for all the world to see Him in you. You weren't created for you; you were created for Him, for His purpose, for His use. You were intended to be a tool in His hands, a weapon, if you will, something He can use to tear down the world of darkness, something He can use to make the enemy quiver and shake in fear.

God wants to use you as a person whose sole desire is God Himself, because when your sole desire is God, you become unstoppable and reckless (in a good way). You have much to accomplish. The dreams and goals God has placed in you aren't by accident or coincidence. They were thought of by God Himself, placed in you by His very hand and by His wisdom. Don't let jealousy or competition get in the way.

This race isn't about who looks the best or who has the most talents or gifts. It's about GOD. Jesus said, *"the Son of Man came not to be served but to serve,"* (Matthew 20:28). So, serve God. Do what He says, when He says. Serve people. Think of others more than of yourself. Stop thinking it's all about you because it's never been about YOU.

Don't disregard the mountain-sized dreams you have. They were given to you by God. Know that they are unattainable without Him. Know that without character, your calling is tainted. Do what's right behind closed doors. Build character before you build your dreams. CONCENTRATE, FOR YOUR CALLING IS GREAT!

DAY 11

THE SECRET PLACE

There's no greater place to hear the voice of God than in "the secret place." The secret place is your alone time with God. It's the place where no one else is watching. The true test of a man or a woman is what they do behind closed doors. For the Christian, it's the place of intimacy with God, and it's the place of promotion.

Intimacy is an act that God created to be enjoyed between a man and a woman within the confines of marriage. Intimacy with God happens much in the same way. In your constant pursuit of God, the relationship goes further and gets deeper. Just like a boyfriend and a girlfriend, there are stages of knowing the other person until you get to the point of marriage. When you spend alone time with God, He lets you know Him, and because He is God, you will never stop knowing Him.

There's a story in the Bible in which Jesus tells about a man who finds himself before God at the end of his life. It's judgment time, and the man pleads for his place in eternity. He states that he has done miracles in God's name, cast out demons in God's name, and prophesied in God's name. However, the Father responds, *"I never knew you; depart from Me, you workers of lawlessness,"* (Matthew 7:23). Jesus paints this chilling picture of a man who knew all the "church lingo," who was most likely in church, who did miracles and who had gifts of the Spirit. There was one key ingredient he was missing: KNOWING.

This man was a version of our modern-day Christian, attending church services, but not really knowing God during the week. The man played a part, but He didn't know the Creator. He pursued the gifts instead of the Giver. He was lacking relationship.

Relationships are always built on time. Every day, when you get home, you have options. You can do anything you'd like, but there's something special about the person who can do anything, yet chooses to meet with God. He or she could get on social media, play video games, hang with friends, watch TV, watch Netflix, open a laptop, or do anything else that came to mind, but instead they choose to spend time with God.

God prefers *you* more than what you can do for Him. When you have your alone time with God, whether it be reading the Bible, listening for His voice, or singing to Him in worship, you are knowing God intimately.

There's an infinite amount of ways you can spend your alone time with God, but there doesn't have to be an exact way. Simply spend time with Him alone. Open your Bible and ask Him to reveal Himself to you. Put your headphones on and play music that glorifies Him and sing along to Him. Sit in the darkness of your room and experience Him. Invite Him, verbally, into whatever space you decide to be with Him in, and watch Him change the atmosphere. Speak to Him, and then listen. Allow Him to be God. Build a relationship. KNOW HIM! KNOW HIM! KNOW HIM!

DAY 12

PERFECTION

Perfection is a process. Many will tell you that you can never be perfect, but I'm here to tell you otherwise. Perfection is attainable, and you should aim for it. Jesus Himself commanded us, *"But you are to be perfect, even as your Father in heaven is perfect,"* (Matthew 5:48, NLT). WHAT DID HE SAY? That's right, Jesus implied that we can be perfect.

Jesus didn't stop there. He went on to say, "BE perfect." Naysayers will tell you it's blasphemy, it's pride, and it's unattainable, but I would rather take God's Word than man's. I agree with Jesus. So, be perfect!

What does that mean? It means getting to a place of falling so in love with God that you develop something called "character." You do what's right when no one's looking. You pray for people who hurt you. You lend without expecting to be repaid. You possess the fruits of the Spirit. You're gentle and understanding. You're calm yet confident. God's desires become your desires. Sin becomes distasteful to you. In fact, it becomes disgusting to you. You love people that hate you. You spend time with God, and you involve God in everything you do constantly throughout your day.

You're relentless. You're focused. You're passionate. You can be perfect. It doesn't mean you'll never mess up, and it doesn't mean you're always going to be absolutely sinless. It does mean that you'll be resilient. Resilience is being able to withstand or recover quickly from difficult conditions. This means that even if you mess up, you get right back into shape, right back into having character and integrity. You may slip, but it won't continue. You bounce back quickly. The old version of you may have gone off into a series of failures and a lengthy drought, but that won't be you anymore. You're going to be different. You're going to be outstanding, sincere, and pure.

I want to challenge you. Do something out of the box. Perfection is God's quality, and God's qualities can only be developed in you when you pursue Him. So do something new and crazy. Ask God how many hours each day would be a good amount of time for you to be intimate with Him. Then make it a daily goal not to go to bed until you've accomplished the particular amount of time you need to reach Him. Your relationship with God will grow, and your character will reflect it. Watch everything change. Be perfect, as He is perfect!

DAY 13

DELIVERANCE

From the beginning of time, there have been options, options to do right or wrong—choices, if you will. God gave Adam and Eve an option. He allowed them to eat from most trees, but He forbid them from eating the fruit from one particular tree. Adam and Eve had options.

As the story goes on, we discover that disobedience came into the world, which also created sin. Sin is choosing the wrong option. Sin created distance between God and man. God didn't run away, but sin caused man to feel dirty, shameful, and naked. Sin caused man to run from God, and beyond that, sin created a wedge between a perfect God and imperfect humans. So, something was needed; Someone was needed.

Years passed, and it became a practice for people to sacrifice animals in order to pay a price for their sins, to be clean before God and be forgiven. There came a point when God became so desperate for relationship with man that He no longer wanted the barrier of sin to have any power. The only issue was how could that even be possible? People would sacrifice certain animals to demonstrate how great their remorse and repentance was, but no animal was great enough to bring permanent forgiveness. They would sacrifice yearly for their sins, but go on sinning.

One day, God sent His amazing and sinless Son, Jesus Christ, into the world with one purpose: to save people by giving them a relationship with God that had no limits and no need for sacrifices. Jesus had to live perfectly so that when He sacrificed His body physically, it would be a perfect sacrifice. Through that sacrifice, He paid the price that you and I should have paid. His sacrifice makes it as if you had never messed up. That doesn't mean you should live however you want; it means you should realize what He did for you, fall in love with Him, and live as He would live.

The Bible says, *"For the Son of Man came to seek and to save that which was lost,"* (Luke 19:10). If you want to know your purpose in life, look at Jesus' life and imitate Him. As a Christian, we're called to save other people. Jesus left the Earth, but the Bible says that He now lives in us (if you've accepted Him, of course). So, He lives in us and desires to use us to save and deliver others.

Everywhere you go, there's a chance that you'll be around someone who has no relationship with God. You have the amazing truth inside you that the world needs to hear. As you build God's voice in your daily life, you're going to begin to hear Him speak to you in everyday situations. You may be at the grocery store, and God could nudge you to speak to a complete stranger and tell them that He loves them. A statement as simple as that could create a conversation that changes a person's eternity.

Today, realize that God wants to use you anywhere and everywhere. Overcome the fear of approaching people you don't know. Listen for God's voice in everyday life. You may be the only version of Jesus that someone ever sees.

DAY 14

POWER

The power of the tongue is often overlooked. The tongue has an amazing ability to speak and create. The Bible says, in the book of Hebrews, *"By faith we understand that the universe was created by the word of God, so that what is seen was not made out of things that are visible,"* (Hebrews 11:3). God enjoys doing things that don't make sense to the human mind. He creates the physical by using something that is invisible: WORDS! So, there is power in words, even though we cannot see them. You can create your present and your future by what you say.

In the same way that God created light by speaking (see Genesis), we can create today by using words. The Bible says, *"Death and life are in the power of the tongue, and those who love it will eat its fruits,"* (Proverbs 18:21). In other words, you're bound by what you say, positively or negatively. Your tongue can create, form, destroy, build up, or even tear down.

For example, God told Jeremiah, *"Behold, I have put My words in your mouth. See, I have appointed you today over nations and kingdoms to uproot and tear down, to destroy and overthrow, to build and plant,"* (Jeremiah 1:9-10, BSB). The question God has for you is this: "What words are you speaking? And what kind of future are you creating?"

The Bible tells us in the book of James that the tongue is humanly impossible to tame. It refers to the tongue as a restless evil, and it goes on to say that the tongue is like a rudder. A very tiny rudder can control the direction of a huge ship, depending on where the pilot is directing it. Much like the pilot of a ship, you're the pilot of your life, and your tongue directs where you go. Yes, the Bible says that we cannot tame the tongue, but there is one exception to that rule. What if you were surrendered so completely to God that you allowed Him to become the pilot of your life?

The tongue is impossible to tame by any human, but when that human tells God, "God, I am nothing without You, and I surrender my life and my will to You; do with me whatever You want," at that point He begins to take control of your "rudder," He begins to put His voice in you, and He begins to control you.

The Bible says, *"it is God who works in you, both to will and to work for His good pleasure,"* (Philippians 2:3). God wants to create His future in you and in others, and the only way He can do that is through His voice. As you listen *for* God and *to* God, His words will begin to build something in you. In order to hear God's voice consistently and clearly you must make a daily habit of reading His written Word. This Word is essential to being able to hear the voice of God.

As you read the Bible, God will instill and inject within you faith, hope, boldness, confidence, trust, and the rest of the awesome qualities He has prepared for you. Reading and speaking the Bible out loud will help to develop in you the characteristics and the traits you need to live a powerful, fulfilling, walk with God.

Surrender today! Allow God to become the pilot of your life, and watch your destiny begin to form as He creates it with His voice.

SEEKING

In order to develop the voice of God in your life, you have to learn how to SEEK. To seek is to attempt to find. One of my all-time favorite verses in the Bible is Jeremiah 33:3, *"Call to Me and I will answer you, and will tell you great and hidden things that you have not known."* There is a reward for seeking God, and the reward is finding Him!

The first time I ever heard God's voice was when I was fifteen years old and playing a video game. I heard internally, like a thought, "Read the Bible," but I knew it wasn't my own thought. I knew it wasn't my voice. God allowed me to understand that it was Him communicating with me. From that day on, I began to increase my time with God, running to do whatever He would impress on me when He would speak to me. The more you obey God's nudging and voice in your life, the stronger His voice will become, and the deeper will be the things He tells you.

The Bible tells us, *"Seek the LORD while He may be found; call upon Him while He is near,"* (Isaiah 55:6). On one particular night, that verse was put to the test in my life. I was at home with my three older brothers and my parents, having what seemed like an ordinary movie night. Probably about halfway through the movie, I heard God speak to me. It was in a tone I had never heard God speak to me before. He told me very clearly and strongly, "If you love Me, go to your room."

I thought for a moment, "If I don't go, that means I don't love God." I told my family I had to go to my room, but I didn't say why. I ran to my room, closed the door, and turned off the lights. I realized that God was calling me, so I wanted to find Him. I grabbed my headphones and cellphone and went on YouTube and put a Christian worship song on. Then I got on my knees, lifted my hands to God, and began singing in my room to Him.

Within fifteen seconds, I suddenly felt God's presence like a jolt of electricity. I first felt it on my left hand, and then the feeling began to move through my whole body until I felt Him all over me. I started crying deeply, and I could feel God loving me. I remember thinking to myself, "What if I had stayed on that couch and thought that it was too crazy for God to speak to me?" I would've missed out on the most amazing moment in my life.

God is looking for people to do things out of the ordinary, to believe that He can do anything, and to believe that He would do anything just to be with us. *"You will seek Me and find Me, when you seek Me with all your heart,"* (Jeremiah 29:13).

FRUITS

The absolute greatest qualities you could possibly possess in life are the fruits of the Spirit: *"Love, joy, peace, patience, kindness, goodness, faithfulness, gentleness, self-control,"* (Galatians 5:22-23). These are qualities that you can't get anywhere else but by being with God. Jesus said, *"I am the vine and you are the branches. The one who remains in Me, and I in him, will bear much fruit. For apart from Me you can do nothing,"* (John 15:5, BSB). The fruits are a vital part of your walk with God, because they are proof that you have been with God, and they are tools that God uses to show the world what He looks like.

The Bible says that Christians will be known by their love, so how you carry yourself is proof of who you are and Who you belong to. The Bible even tells us to judge a tree (a person) by its fruit (their characteristics) (see Matthew 7:16). If you want to identify the kind of fruits you possess (or someone else possess), then analyze the difficult moments. The test of a man and of a woman is not in the good times, but in the bad times. Look for reactions. By seeing the way you react to bad moments, I can tell you the kind of fruits you possess.

Fruits are very hard to develop because they require you to slow down in life. Every time you get into your alone time with God, you are saying "no" to everyone and everything else. So it's costly; it's not easy. God asks something of you—your time, your surrender. That's why it's so hard to find someone filled with the fruits of the Spirit; it requires a sacrifice. The more you take time to be alone with God, the more He works on and develops you. Every second you spend with God is a seed you plant in the soil of your life. These seeds will produce invaluable fruit.

How many fruits do you have?

How do you react to bad situations?

Aim to develop spiritual fruits, and you'll become unstoppable. The enemy cannot phase a Christian who is filled with the fruits of the Spirit. So, I challenge you to be different today! Love those who hate you! Bless those who curse you! Pray for those who do you wrong!

Go the extra mile! Be gentle! Be courteous! Think of others more than of yourself! Be patient! Be faithful! Most importantly, be alone with God, and watch how everything about you will change!

PROMISES

The Bible tells us that the promises of God are *"Yes"* and *"amen"* (2 Corinthians 1:20, NLT). This means that God will fully deliver on everything He has promised you. The Scriptures tell us that God holds His Word even above His name (see Psalm 138:2). He sees greater value in what He says than in Himself. Why? Because anyone who doesn't keep their word devalues the integrity of their name.

One of the most amazing aspects of hearing God's voice is the sole fact that you can guarantee that what He said to you He will certainly do. This can be extremely reassuring and help instill confidence.

Up until the age of twenty-two, I was terrified of speaking in front of people. Then, one night I confronted that old fear to preach, and God removed it all in an instant. Once God removed it, the enemy's next attack was through thoughts that God wouldn't use me. I was preparing to preach one night, and I heard God say to me, "Every time you go to speak, preach, and pray, I'm going to speak, preach, and pray through you." This statement let me know that God would never let me down. He would fill my mouth with words every time. This gave me a confidence that nothing else could give.

God's promises trump the voice of the devil. Regardless of what the devil throws at you or says about you, he cannot destroy what God has set in motion. What God speaks happens. There's no question about it. It's set in stone. You can take every promise that God has ever given you to the bank.

The promises in the Bible are no exception. Remind yourself constantly of what God has already said to you in His Word. Recite those promises! Declare them! Shout them out, for they will surely come to pass. Habakkuk 2:2-3 says, *"And the Lord answered me: 'Write the vision; make it plain on tablets, so he may run who reads it. For still the vision awaits its appointed time; it hastens to the end—it will not lie. If it seems slow, wait for it; it will surely come; it will not delay.'"* Speak God's promises and write them out. They will surely come to pass.

HEALING

A woman in the Bible had been suffering from an issue of blood for twelve years, and no one had been able to help her. She was frustrated, tired and helpless, but she decided to give it one last try—one last push for healing. Hearing that Jesus was passing nearby, she made up her mind that if she could just touch His garment, she would be healed. And that's exactly what happened. She pushed her way through the crowd, reached out and touched Jesus' garment. The Bible says that He immediately felt virtue leaving His body, and the woman was instantly healed!

There are many forms of healing: physical, emotional, mental, and spiritual, just to name a few. Everyone has needed healing at some point in life, and God wants to use you, much like His garment, as a tool He can flow through to instantly change the lives of other people. Sometimes God will speak to you to lead you or direct you to a specific person, and sometimes He'll just reveal to you that if you pray for anyone, He'll show up.

One day I went to the gym and saw my friend Jorge getting ready to leave. We made eye contact, and I went to greet him. When I asked how he was doing, he answered, "Man, you won't believe it. I got diagnosed with thyroid cancer. They removed my thyroid, but they said there's still cancer remaining and I'm going to need radiation. They told me I won't be able to live a normal life anymore." He was worried because he had children. He would miss his workouts and he was terrified of having to get radiation.

As Jorge was telling me all this, I heard the Holy Spirit speak to me: "Pray for him, and I'll heal him." I said, "Man, I'm so sorry, bro. I'm a Christian. Is it okay if I pray for you? I believe that Jesus can heal you." He responded, "Yeah, man, you can pray for me."

My prayer wasn't long. I rebuked the spirit of cancer and commanded all cancer to leave Jorge's body in Jesus' name. As he was thanking me for the prayer, God spoke to me again. I heard Him say, "Tell him there's no more cancer in his body, and he's not going to need radiation." Wow! THAT WAS A BOLD STATEMENT! But I trusted God, so I said it, word for word.

A month later, I was arriving at the gym, and as I was looking for a parking spot, I saw Jorge walking to his car to leave. He saw me and signaled me to wait for him. I parked, and he came up to my window. He said, "Man, I went to the doctor a couple weeks ago for a checkup, and I asked if there was any possible way I could get out of taking the radiation. The doctor tested me, checked the results, then went back to look at the results a second time. When she came back, she looked at me and said, 'There is ZERO cancer in your body, and you don't need radiation anymore. You can go back to living the way you used to live.'"

I was amazed. "YOU SEE HOW AMAZING GOD IS!" I said. Jorge looked at me and then said something that will stick with me forever: "I didn't know that God could answer prayers outside of church." "He did that to show you how MUCH He loves you," I responded.

You have to understand: Jorge wasn't a regular church attender. He didn't earn that miracle. Healing is a way God shows people He's real and that He loves them.

Allow God to use you as a tool to love other people. It doesn't have to be just physical healing. It can be anything that anyone needs in that moment. Make yourself available by listening for God's voice on a constant basis. His voice will lead you to powerful prayers and moments that will forever change the lives of other people. Get ready! He's about to use you!

Distractions

YOU WILL ENCOUNTER DISTRACTIONS, many of them. It's a part of the process, and it's a part of the game. The enemy will hit you in so many ways it will astound you, but it doesn't mean you have to give in to him. The enemy will throw people, situations, attitudes, and problems at you, to make you uncomfortable, unwilling to go on, tired of fighting, and sick of the race called "life."

A distraction is anything or anyone that is not part of God's plan for your life or deters you from God's will. Distractions will cloud your ability to hear God, so run from them. They will delay you, delay your destiny, and delay your calling. Most importantly, distractions will hinder your relationship with God, a price that is never worth risking.

So, how do you fight distractions? How do you get rid of them? You absolutely have to attack them. In the story of David and Goliath, we see a young man who knew God and had a deep relationship with Him. Goliath was a distraction and an example to us today of the distractions we face in life. Every day, for forty days, Goliath would come out to taunt God and His people Israel, and they were terrified. It is important that you recognize how the devil speaks in order to beat him at his own game. One of the devil's languages is distractions.

David was different. He was humble, intimate with God, and had fought battles that no one else knew about. Your closeness to God will determine the strength with which you attack the distractions in your life. It's hard to attack distractions when you neglect your alone time with God. A man or a woman who is focused on being close, intimate, and deep with God will overcome any mountain, any enemy, and any storm.

Don't let distractions get in the way. Recognize them quickly. Distractions will pull you away from God. They can be jobs, friendships, relationships, or addictions. Eliminate them by doing exactly what David and Jesus did. Use your words against them! Jesus had Satan running in defeat after He was tempted for forty days and nights. Satan quoted scriptures to distract Jesus, but Jesus used Satan's very own tactic. He hit him back immediately with the Word of God. When you speak, God creates. So tell Satan who God is and who you are in Him.

The stone David threw was a representation of Jesus, the Cornerstone. The five stones he picked up were a revelation of God's grace. So, likewise, God will give you the grace to hit your enemy with the stone that is intimacy with Jesus Christ.

David made one last move to eliminate his enemy. The final step is the cutting off of the head of your distraction. Jesus said, *"And if your right hand causes you to sin, cut it off and throw it away. For it is better that you lose one of your members than that your whole body go into hell,"* (Matthew 5:30). You must eliminate the voice of the distraction in your life. Identify the avenue through which you're being attacked and cut off its path.

If you're struggling with certain addictions because of wrong influences, cut off those wrong relationships. No matter where or how you're being distracted, there is always a way to cut off the voice of that distraction. Destroy your giant today by eliminating his voice. Go for the throat of your distraction, and conquer it once and for all.

DAY 20

OVERCOMING

You cannot learn how to truly overcome until you've faced a situation that you can't control. It's called TRUST. There are moments in our lives we haven't anticipated and moments we couldn't plan for.

One of the ways that God speaks is through His peace. It's a feeling of confirmation from God that you're doing His will and that you're in the right. More importantly, it's an assurance that God's going to take care of you. A lack of peace is a strong indicator of warning, disobedience, or correction. As you open your mind to the reality that God wants to speak to you in different ways, He will then enhance your ability to hear and recognize His voice.

The Bible tells us, *"So whether you eat or drink or whatever you do, do it all for the glory of God,"* (1 Corinthians 10:31, NIV). As you involve God in everything you do, He will develop trust in your life. In order to overcome hard moments, you have to trust God's voice. The key ingredient to getting out of a season of hardship is obedience. So, how can you hear God's voice throughout your day? By involving Him in everything you do.

One of the habits God has given me is to ask Him for His input before I take on any task. Why? God isn't just looking for you to inquire of Him in your large decisions; He's looking for you to involve Him in all of your decisions. He wants to show you that He will bless what you give Him. The reason why Matthew 6:33 is so effective is because of it's first command: *"SEEK FIRST the kingdom of God... ."* When you commit to God what you're about to do, you're proving to Him that you trust Him. You're saying, "God, You can do this better than I can. In fact, I can't do this at all, and You can."

Trust and obedience go hand-in-hand. When you obey, you trust. In order for you to fully trust God, He must have full control. Today, allow God to develop trust in your life. Before you go to work, ask Him to help you with your workload and to give you wisdom. Before you go to school, commit your exams and studying to God by praying before you do your assignments. There is nothing too small for God to be concerned with.

Involve God in the little things as well as the great, and He'll begin to speak to you in everything you do. As you trust God with your small moments, He will give you strength for your greatest trials. You won't overcome tough situations because you know how to pray, nor because you attend church every week. You will overcome tough situations because you trust that God's voice will always carry you through your lowest valley.

DAY 21

FORGIVENESS

There are hindrances to hearing the voice of God, and one of the greatest is a failure to forgive others. The Bible says, *"But if you do not forgive, neither will your Father who is in heaven forgive your offenses,"* (Mark 11:26, NASB). WHAT A SCARY STATEMENT! Jesus displayed forgiveness in the most beautiful way. He demonstrated the way we ought to be in hard circumstances and in good ones. We are to be the same regardless of what comes against us.

Character is not how good you are in good moments, but how good you are in all moments. Jesus was heard saying to those who mocked Him while hanging on the cross, *"Father, forgive them for they know not what they do,"* (Luke 23:34). What a powerful and beautiful statement. Imagine forgiving not only those who are making fun of you, but also those who are putting you to death. Imagine forgiving someone who was killing you and doing it while they were in the process.

Forgiveness was given by God to all of us. We've done way worse to God than anyone has ever done to us, yet He forgave us, He loved us, and He has never changed with us. God is merely asking that we give to others what He's given to us: mercy, grace, compassion, salvation, and FORGIVENESS.

It is important to know that it doesn't matter if the person who has wronged you apologizes or if they ever change. The

Bible doesn't say to forgive people if they apologize to you. It doesn't say be good to people if they're good to you. God's forgiveness is such that regardless of what you did and how you did it, He's going to forgive you with no strings attached and will hold nothing against you.

Today, develop the forgiveness of God. Forgive people, forget their wrongs, and let go of the past that you've held against them. Unforgiveness will eat away at you physically, emotionally, and spiritually. What a scary thought it is that God cannot forgive me if I fail to forgive those who have sinned against me! And what a tragedy to treat someone else any other way than with the compassion and love that God has shown me! Forgiveness is one of the greatest qualities you can possess! When you display it, you are truly displaying the love of God!

Day 22

Faith

The Bible says that faith is the substance of things hoped for, the evidence of things not seen (see Hebrews 11:1). Faith cannot be understood, and it cannot be fathomed. If you want to understand faith, it will never happen. However, if you believe, anything can happen.

Jesus tells us that nothing is impossible for them that believe (see Matthew 17:20). So today, I'm asking you one favor. Can you believe with all that you are that God wants to be intimate with you, that He cares about every aspect of your life and that He absolutely wants to speak to you?

Physical evidence is simple, and it's easy to believe something that you see, but there's no great reward for believing the physical realm. There *is* such a reward when you sing to a God you cannot see and speak to a God you cannot see. When He touches you, speaks to you, and allows you to feel His presence, there is no longer a doubt in your mind that He exists.

God then causes you to pursue Him even further, because you now realize that He works in the realm of uncertainty. He likes to show up when things don't make sense. He likes to touch you when you can't see anything. Why? Because He knows the price you paid to even believe that He exists. You love God so much that you are going out on a limb to believe He's even there. This causes you to pursue Him even further.

The Bible tells us, *"Without faith it is impossible to please God, because anyone who comes to Him must believe that He exists and that He rewards those who earnestly seek Him,"* (Hebrews 11:6, NIV). There is a prize for going to church. There is a prize for reading your Bible. There is a prize for doing the right thing when you think no one's looking. There is a prize for singing to God. There is a prize for spending time alone with God. And that prize … is God Himself.

It would be easy to worship God if you could physically see Him. It takes a much stronger person to pursue a God they can't see. That's why God chose to make the reward something tangible, out of something that is invisible. It's why He created the world with His words. It's why He created day and night with His very words. He enjoys using the invisible, because faith will push you harder toward God once you've had a glimpse of Him.

"Taste and see that the Lord is good," (Psalm 34:8, NIV). You cannot taste God until you've used faith, for without faith it is impossible to please God!

DAY 23

HEARING

Jesus said, *"Ask, and you will receive,"* (John 16:24, NKJV). The key to hearing God is one word found in this very verse: *ASK*! The moment I realized that God wants to speak to us, my desire for His voice increased dramatically. I began to ask God about everything.

When I was about nineteen, I was standing in front of my pantry one day, and the thought came to me that God cares about absolutely everything I did. I was hungry for God's voice, so I dared to believe that He could speak to me about anything. Instead of picking a cereal to eat that day, as I normally did, I said, "Holy Spirit, what cereal do You want me to eat?" Then I quieted myself and waited for Him to speak or indicate His desire.

This moment, while it may seem crazy or small to you, meant everything to Him. He used the quality of faith in me to produce His constant voice in me. You, too, can have as much of God as you want, and He can get as deep as you want, depending on how far you allow Him to go. If you want to hear God's voice, pursue Him! Run after Him! Desire Him, and don't be halfway! Make the decision that you're going to give God all of you, regardless of what He does.

One night, in my alone time with God, I was worshipping Him with my headphones on and the lights off, and I experienced one of the most intense moments of God's presence. Even after I took my headphones off, I felt so close to Him that I just wanted to lie down and hear Him speak. So, I did exactly that. I lay down and asked God, "God, what do you have for me to do?" I immediately heard a response from God in my head, "Go get your drink."

A few days prior to this, I had been craving a certain Japanese *boba* drink, and I understood that this was what God was referring to. My initial response was, "But, God, I'm in Your presence. I don't want to get a drink. I want to be with You." Then God's voice got even stronger in my head, and He gave me a pounding response, "Go get your drink! Go get your drink! Go get your drink!" I couldn't get Him to change His answer, so I finally obeyed.

I got up, got dressed, and headed to the location. There were no customers in the store, only two female employees. I headed to the counter, and one of the ladies asked me what flavor I wanted. I said, "What flavors do you have?" She said, "There's a menu in the back of the store." As I was walking to the back of the store, God spoke to me again and said, "Tell her that I love her." After making my order, I said, "Do you know Jesus?" She responded, "I knew of Him as a little girl, but not really since then." I said, "He told me to tell you that He loves you very much, and He has a great destiny and plan for you."

She wiped tears from her face, as she said to me, "For the last five days I've been debating if I should go back to church. I haven't been there since I was about six. Because you came and talked to me, I'm going to go back." SHE HADN'T BEEN TO CHURCH IN OVER THIRTY YEARS!

I looked at my drink, then I looked at her and said, "God didn't send me for this drink; He sent me here for you." He knew that for the last five days this woman had debated going back to church, and He wanted to use me to get to her and change her life forever. How powerful God is! How beautiful it is to hear His voice! How necessary it is to hear His voice! Your willingness to listen to God's voice could change another person forever, better yet, for all eternity.

WILDERNESS

The wilderness is the place where you learn to depend upon the Holy Spirit. Jesus had this moment as recorded in Matthew 4. The wilderness is a place where you may feel lonely. There may be no one around. You may feel hopeless, unless you realize that God orchestrated this moment for you and Him to become intimate.

Sometimes God will remove people from your life. Sometimes God will make you change locations. Sometimes God will shift everything, because if He hadn't, you would have missed your destiny.

I have to make something very clear to you: if your end goal in life is your calling or your future, then you've missed it. The end goal and the main goal is (and should always be) intimacy with God, closeness to Him, faithfulness to Him, and knowing how much He really loves you. The whole point to life is GOD. He's it. He's everything. Your calling is worth nothing if you don't know God's voice. Being used by God is worth nothing unless you actually know Him and have a deep relationship with Him.

God is worth everything: the lonely nights, people talking about you, people falsely accusing you, heartbreaks, disappointments, setbacks, etc. He's worth every price you'll ever have to pay.

Jesus had to spend forty days and nights in the wilderness with the Holy Spirit. This was necessary for Him to find fulfillment in the Holy Spirit. The Bible says that after this period of time, Jesus became hungry, and Satan came to tempt Him. Notice two important keys here:

1. Jesus wasn't hungry during the forty days and nights because He had learned how to be nourished by His relationship with the Holy Spirit.
2. Satan likes to tempt you when your flesh is hungry.

Jesus was craving something, so Satan tried to tempt Him with food, pride, and power. The mistake Satan made was not understanding that Jesus had already discovered the answer of true fulfillment. He had already discovered how to satisfy Himself by the Holy Spirit. His alone time with the Holy Spirit taught Him that His joy, His attention, His peace, His fulfillment, all came from God. The only way Jesus could have discovered that the Holy Spirit can provide all these things was by being alone with Him for a period of time with no one and nothing else around to offer Him anything.

Sometimes God will isolate you in life for a period of time so that you can develop intimacy and closeness to the Holy Spirit. This is so that He can show you that God can meet every need your soul and flesh has; you don't need to look for it anywhere else. You must spend more time in the Word, more time in worship, more time in God's presence, more time listening for His voice, more time being intimate with the Holy Spirit. This will lead you to a happiness no one else could ever give you. It is necessary to develop this before God takes you into your destiny.

Immediately after Jesus became intimate with the Holy Spirit and He rejected Satan's attempts to tempt Him, the Father placed Jesus into His calling! Jesus began His ministry after surpassing the wilderness with the Holy Spirit.

DAY 25

PRUNING

Everyone has to go through hard circumstances. The question is: What do you do in hard circumstances? Jesus, in John 15, spoke of the parable in which His Father is the gardener, He Himself is the vine, and we are the branches. He gives this beautiful illustration that simplifies the Gospel and the whole point of life.

The Father is responsible for tending to us as a gardener. Jesus had to be submissive and allow the Gardener to do what He wanted, and we receive life by being attached to the vine that is Jesus. Jesus then revealed that unless we abide and live and dwell in Him, we cannot produce something called "fruit." Next He said, *"Every branch in me that does not bear fruit He takes away, and every branch that does bear fruit He prunes, that it may bear more fruit,"* (John 15:2). So pruning is a necessity for displaying fruit in your life.

The definition of *pruning* is "to trim by cutting away dead or overgrown branches, especially to increase fruitfulness and growth." The moment you possess one good fruit, God decides it's necessary to cut some things off of you that were dead so that you will become even more fruitful. You have to allow God to work on you in hard situations by training you to respond correctly. Every time you encounter a difficult situation, you're being tested, to see if you have any fruits. Testing is a good sign because it means you're about to produce something great. God's about to create something in you that you didn't have before.

You've had to endure heartbreaks. You've had to encounter shortcomings. You've had to go through horrible situations. Why? One day those situations (the ones you thought you'd never make it out of) will release a seed, to produce a fruit that you would never have developed had it not been for that hard situation. Difficult situations should never kill you, nor slow you down. Difficult situations should make you into who God has always wanted you to be.

REJECTION

In your walk with God, one of the things you will certainly encounter is rejection. People will talk about you, mistreat you, talk to you ugly, use you, and even get angry that you live for Jesus. The Bible tells us, *"God blesses you when people mock you and persecute you and lie about you and say all sorts of evil things against you because you are My followers,"* (Matthew 5:11, NLT). Get happy when people talk about you! How's that for a new mindset?

What if you realized that everything bad that has ever happened to you is used by God for your good? What if you didn't care about what other people thought about you? I want you to reject the feeling of rejection. I want you to embrace the lifestyle that nothing can touch you, deter you, nor harm you.

When you're truly living for God, nothing can stop you. The Bible says that Jesus was rejected, yet He still died for everyone. He still loved those who hated Him. He loved those who mistreated Him.

To reject something or someone is to dismiss or refuse them. Today, dismiss the ability to be rejected. Refuse the ability to be offended. When God has accepted you, no man can reject you. When God works everything together for your good, you can remove worry from the equation.

As God enables you to unlock His voice in your life, He will use you as His mouthpiece—His voice to the world. Not everyone will accept you, but not everyone will reject you. Become determined that nothing that is thrown against you will change who you are inside. Remain steadfast in doing good. Be constant in being faithful. If people reject you, love them. If they talk about you, don't talk about them. Be different! Be resilient! Be steadfast! Be open! Be forgiving! Be gentle! As you do this, you are becoming more and more like Jesus.

DAY 27

Hate

There is a place for hatred, but it must be harnessed. Hatred is good when you use it in the right direction. Jesus said, *"If anyone comes to Me and does not hate his own father and mother and wife and children and brothers and sisters, yes, and even his own life, he cannot be My disciple,"* (Luke 14:26). Did Jesus just say hate? Yes, He did. What did He mean? There is a reference in the Bible to two masters, and how we must choose the one we will serve. Jesus said, *"You will either hate one and love the other, or you will be devoted to one and despise the other,"* (Matthew 6:24, NIV). Jesus was saying that you have two options. There are two masters available in your life: God or anything and everything else. Being devoted to someone is to be faithful at all costs. So Jesus was saying that we must develop a hatred, not a literal one, but a hatred for not being devoted to Him.

God does not want to rule you as a slave, but He wants a relationship with you as a Father. There is something beautiful about the mentality that says, "I'm going to love God at all costs. I'm going to be faithful to Him. I'm going to do what He says. I'm going to go where He says to go." Devotion will take you to places you could never have otherwise imagined. Devotion will save you from heartbreaks. Devotion will save you from setbacks. Devotion will make you or break you. So, God says, we must HATE the other master.

The other master is the one that tells you to do whatever you want, that tells you to go back to your old lifestyle, that tells you to hang out with the wrong influences, and that tells you do whatever feels good in the moment. There are two masters, whether we realize it or not, every day of our lives. God is asking that we merely choose Him, that we would simply love and be devoted to one master–to Him.

One of the greatest keys to hearing God's voice is making the daily decision to choose to live the way He would want you to. Obedience is key in every season of your life. Your devotion to God will cause His voice to become clearer and clearer. So, make the right decisions, and watch His voice increase.

Stillness

Sometimes we have to stop everything just to get closer to God. Life gets in the way ... if you let it. Things like friends, hobbies, adventures, work, careers, and time in general are all a part of life, but they can be very dangerous when they take you away from God. I am not saying you cannot have both; I'm saying that it's easy to allow one to get in the way of the other.

The Bible says, *"Be still, and know that I am God. I will be exalted among the nations, I will be exalted in the earth!"* (Psalm 46:10). Stillness is your ability to cancel out everything else and "zone in" on one thing. God is looking for your focus. A single-minded focus for Him is what He desires. Anything can get in the way. Obsession is an idea or thought that continually preoccupies or intrudes on a person's mind.

Have you ever been in a church service, and your mind continuously wandered? Maybe you have trouble paying attention for a long time. Or maybe it is extremely difficult for you to have personal alone time with God at home, because you can't seem to focus? This is because something or someone has been occupying your mind, because you've been giving it or them the majority of your time. When you rule out things or people you normally spend time with, to increase your time with God, your focus begins to change.

If you feel distracted, it's because you are. There's no better way to solve a problem in your relationship with God than being completely open and honest. This was the reason God called David, in the Bible, *"A man after his [God's] own heart,"* (1 Samuel 13:14, NLT). It wasn't because David was perfect; it was because David desired to please God. He always spoke to God from his heart. David told God the good and the bad.

Stillness can be good or bad. Everyone utilizes the gift of stillness every day. The questions are, "Who or what captures your attention?" and "Who or what has your focus?" You can get so busy with life, so distracted. Someone can have your attention to the point that it costs you your calling, your intimacy with God, your closeness to God, and your passion with Him. It can cost you your relationship with God. Ask yourself if what you're longing for is more important than God Himself. Is it worth losing God?

FIRE

The fire of God is created to take you to a new level. It serves many purposes. Do not run from the fire. It is necessary for your growth. The fire of God cleanses, purifies, burns, enhances, promotes, ignites, and creates something within the soul of every person that makes him- or herself available to God.

There is a famous story in the Bible of a physical fire. There were three young Hebrew men, Shadrach, Meshach, and Abednego, who stood up to King Nebuchadnezzar, a powerful man who was opposed to God. The king ordered the men to be thrown into a fiery furnace because they had been disobedient to his command to bow down to a golden statue. These three men took a stand for God, when the rest of the nation did not.

After giving the men a second chance, the king then ordered them to be bound, and he ordered his workers to turn up the fire seven times hotter than normal. What he didn't know was that seven is God's number. In other words, the hotter fire was God's plan all along.

After the three men were thrown into the furnace, something amazing happened. A fourth person appeared in the fire with them, and absolutely no harm came to the men whatsoever. When King Nebuchadnezzar saw that the men were unharmed, he praised their God and acknowledged that He was the one true

God. He then commanded the whole nation to worship only this God.

God knows the trials you're going through even before you go through them. He's seen your future. He's seen your past. But He tests your present moments. He wants to see if you'll stand up in the midst of a generation and a time where most would not stand for God. God will allow you to go through fires in life, to make you who He's always wanted you to be. You cannot make it to the fire of God unless you've made the right decisions.

The three men were thrown into the fire because they rejected sin. They did it to be faithful to God. You will never become who God wants you to be until you've endured trials that are painful, trying, and desperate. You pass tests when you select the correct answers. Stand up for God, even when no one else does. Make the right decisions when no one's looking, for the Father always watches to see who He can promote.

Don't despise the tough moments. They're proof that you've entered the fire of God, and His fire always produces gold. You're being shaped, you're being molded into His image. The fire of God is tangible. Let Him light you on fire so that you will forever burn bright for Him.

THE HOLY SPIRIT

There is absolutely NO ONE like the Holy Spirit. He is so valuable that Jesus said to His disciples, *"Nevertheless, I tell you the truth: it is to your advantage that I go away, for if I do not go away, the Helper will not come to you. But if I go, I will send Him to you,"* (John 16:7). Jesus described the Holy Spirit as being better than Himself! You cannot unlock God's voice without the Holy Spirit. The Bible even describes the Holy Spirit as the deposit and the guarantee of our inheritance, and states that God will do what He promised.

The Holy Spirit has become my best Friend. He leads me, guides me, directs me, and transitions me to where I need to go. Jesus had an intimate moment with the Holy Spirit in Matthew 4, when He was led by the Spirit to be tempted by the devil. Notice that Jesus was led; the Holy Spirit was speaking to Him. Jesus had forty days and nights of alone time with the Holy Spirit. This is an example for us of getting rid of distractions, people, entertainment, food, and anything that can appeal to the flesh. This alone time caused Jesus to be fulfilled by the Holy Spirit. It taught Him to be fed and nourished by the Holy Spirit, but it was not a natural feeding. It was spiritual. The Holy Spirit needed to instill in Jesus the realization that He didn't need anything or anyone to satisfy Him.

The Bible goes on to say that after fasting forty days and nights, Jesus was hungry. He wasn't hungry during the forty days and nights, because He had discovered that His relationship and intimacy with the Holy Spirit fulfilled even His physical needs. The Holy Spirit was the only thing He needed.

Today God is looking for a generation that doesn't depend on what the world depends on to be satisfied. He's looking for a fiery generation that wants Him more than anything else. Your talent and your gifts will never separate you; everyone has them. Your passion, your hunger, and your closeness to God is what will separate you, mark you, and shape you.

Unlocking God's Voice is not just about unlocking any voice. This entire book is not just about hearing His voice; it's completely about *Him*. He's the goal. It's an invitation to be intimate with Him. It's an invitation to be close to Him. It's an invitation to fall in love with Him.

Through this trial, Jesus discovered that there was nothing greater or more fulfilling than His closeness to the Holy Spirit. He had discovered true fulfillment. This book is an invitation to you to fall in love with the Holy Spirit. Invite Him into your life and ask Him to fulfill you. His voice is only proof of the relationship. Simply being with Him is the entire meaning of life. Unlock God's voice, but most importantly, make His heart the goal of your life.

Author Contact Page

You may contact the author directly in the following ways:

www.JeremyRosas.com

Email: jeremymarkrosas@gmail.com

Instagram: Jeremy_Rosas_

Facebook: Jeremy Rosas

YouTube: Unlock God's Voice

TikTok: UnlockGodsVoice

www.ingramcontent.com/pod-product-compliance
Lightning Source LLC
LaVergne TN
LVHW011338080426
835513LV00006B/415